The Negotiator's Playbook - Strategies for Lowering Your Debt and Achieving Financial Freedom
— By Shannon J. Carson And Alex C. Duquette

Copyright © 2023

All Rights Reserved.

No part of this book may be used or reproduced in any manner whatsoever, without the express written permission of the authors.

Table of Contents

Page

So you've Got Bad Debt.

Debt Consolidation, Debt Negotiation & Debt Elimination Companies	12
Debt Negotiation/Settlement	12
Debt Consolidation	13
Debt Elimination	13
Self-Help Debt Negotiation Vs Debt Settlement Company	15
Steps to doing Self-Help Debt Negotiation:	16
Does Self Help Debt Negotiation Work?	17
Steps to Negotiating a Debt Settlement	17
So How Much Should You Offer?	20
Debt Negotiations	21

The Down and Dirty: A Quick Look at How Debt Collection Agencies Operate

The Collector's Advantage	24
An Inside Look - The Collection Agency	25
Junk Debt Buyers	26
Debt Collection Laws	28
Collection Agency Rules	29
Consumer's Rights	30
When to file a complaint	30
Statute of Limitations	31
In Canada	32
In the United States	33

Your Credit Report and YOU!

Getting your Credit Report	36
How to read your credit report.	38

FIGHT BACK!

Tip and tricks, forms and tactics	42
Questions Asked By Collectors	42
Mailing & Record Keeping Instructions	49
Phone Logs	51

The Arsenal

Validation Letter	55
Debt Settlement Letter	56
Paid in Full Letter	58
Debt Payment Agreement Letter	60
Final Payment Warning Letter	62
Payment Refusal and Termination Letter	64
Debt Dispute Letter #1	66
Debt Dispute Letter #2	68
Debt Dispute for New Collector	69
Previously Settled Debt Letter	70
Expired Statute of Limitations Letter	72
Credit Bureau Removal Letter	74
Credit Bureau Removal Follow up Letter	75
BONUS: Sample Opt-Out Letter	76

A Final Word

	79
FREQUENTLY ASKED QUESTIONS	80

Preface

Sometimes, for what ever the reason, we fall behind in our responsibilities to pay our bills. It happens. Regardless, rest assured the creditor will turn the account over to a collection agency and attempt to get the account paid. It is only right that we re-pay what we owe. This program is not about re-paying what we owe. It's about the manner in which the collection agencies and the debt collector go about trying to collect the debt.

While there may be Consumer Protection" guidelines that are in place to protect you from bad actors; in some cases the guidelines are not worth the paper they are written on. I would go further and say those that wrote those guidelines have never had a collector call them or dealt with a collection agency. If they had, many things would be different.

This book will explain many things starting with the beginning of the debt process and ending with clearing up your credit report. This information, you may be familiar with if you have dealt with a debt collector or a collection agency in the past. For many of you this information is new. In either case, the information is true and correct based on my extensive experience as a debt collector with over 30 years of overall knowledge of the collection business.

The purpose of this book is to educate you (the consumer) and provide you with the knowledge to level the playing field when dealing with aggressive debt collectors and collection agencies. Being in debt happens but that does not make you a bad person.

Sometimes debt is over-whelming and the added pressure of an aggressive debt collector only adds to the frustration we already feel. This book will assist you in dealing with your bad debt and help you avoid the idea of bankruptcy or debt consolidation. There are always solutions. Remember..

"Knowledge Is Power"

Shannon J. Carson
CEO of AccuSearch Information Systems, Inc.

Disclaimer

We want to emphasize that the information contained in this book is intended to help consumers become educated about their debt and credit rights. This information is specifically designed to help consumers understand the debt collection process and how to properly dispute debts and credit issues.

However, legal information is not the same as legal advice. We urge you to use caution when using any information contained in this book, including letters, instructions, scripts, opinions, suggestions, and advice. You are strongly encouraged to consult with legal and financial professionals before making any decision that could have legal or financial consequences for you.

The information provided in this book is for educational and informational purposes only. The advice or comments made by the authors of this book are intended only to educate and assist consumers in their own self-help efforts when dealing with debt and credit management issues. It's important to understand that the authors and publishers are not engaged in rendering legal or financial advice or providing credit repair services.

We want to be clear that the information provided should not be used as a substitute for professional counseling and advice from certified legal or financial professionals. While we have made every effort to ensure the accuracy of the information contained herein, based on years of experience in the debt collection and credit process, we cannot be held responsible for any errors or omissions, or for the results obtained from the use of this information.

Please use the information in this book responsibly and consult with a legal or financial professional before making any decisions that could have legal or financial consequences for you.

Best regards,

The Authors,

Shannon J. Carson
Alex C. Duquette

So you've Got Bad Debt.

What do you do? where do you go now?

Debt Consolidation, Debt Negotiation & Debt Elimination Companies

To avoid falling prey to unscrupulous companies that promise to manage your debt, it is essential to understand the differences between debt consolidation, debt negotiation, and debt elimination. Debt consolidation involves taking out a single loan to pay off multiple debts, such as credit card balances or personal loans. This can simplify the payment process and potentially lower the interest rate, but it does not reduce the total amount owed.

Debt negotiation, on the other hand, involves working with a company to negotiate with creditors on your behalf to lower your outstanding balance. This can result in a significant reduction in debt, but it can also have a negative impact on your credit score and may not be successful in all cases. Additionally, debt negotiation companies often charge high fees for their services, which can further exacerbate your financial situation.

Debt elimination is a more extreme option that involves working with a company to settle your debts for less than the full amount owed. This can have a significant impact on your credit score and may not be successful in all cases. Additionally, debt elimination companies often charge high fees and require you to stop making payments to your creditors, which can result in lawsuits and further damage to your credit score.

In summary, it is essential to carefully consider all options and thoroughly research any company before enlisting their services to manage your debt. While debt consolidation, debt negotiation, and debt elimination can all be viable options in certain situations, it is important to weigh the potential benefits and drawbacks of each and make an informed decision that best suits your individual financial needs and circumstances.

Debt Negotiation/Settlement

Debt negotiation or settlement companies may also make unrealistic promises to consumers about the amount of debt they can reduce. These companies often claim that they can significantly reduce a consumer's debt, but in reality, they may only be able to negotiate a small reduction, leaving the consumer with a significant amount of debt remaining. Furthermore, debt negotiation companies may also require consumers to stop making payments to their creditors while negotiations are ongoing. This can lead to missed or late payments, which can negatively impact the consumer's credit score and lead to additional fees and penalties. Overall, debt negotiation or settlement may seem like an attractive option, but consumers should be cautious and thoroughly research any company they are considering working with to avoid falling into a deeper financial hole.

Debt Consolidation

In addition to high fees and interest rates, debt consolidation can also have a negative impact on your credit score. When you consolidate your debts, you are essentially taking out a new loan to pay off your existing debts. This can result in a hard inquiry on your credit report, which can lower your score. Additionally, if you close your credit accounts after consolidating your debt, your credit utilization ratio can also be negatively affected.

Another potential risk of debt consolidation is the temptation to accumulate more debt after consolidating. Since debt consolidation makes it easier to manage monthly payments, some individuals may feel like they have more disposable income and may start using their credit cards again. This can lead to even more debt and financial trouble down the line.

It is important to thoroughly research and compare debt consolidation companies before choosing one to work with. Look for a company with a proven track record of success, reasonable fees and interest rates, and clear and transparent communication. You should also be wary of companies that pressure you into signing up for their services or make unrealistic promises about eliminating your debt quickly and easily.

Debt Elimination

Companies that offer debt elimination rely on many different schemes, but they all hinge on the notion that credit lines are illegal. Debt elimination companies typically provide a document for the lender that supposedly absolves the consumer of the debt, for an upfront fee. Unfortunately, the document has no bearing whatsoever on the debt owed, and consumers paying for such services have found that they've wasted money on a debt elimination scheme that would have been better spent on actually paying back their debt themselves.

Before enlisting the help of a company to manage debt, the Better Business Bureau (BBB) offers the following advice for consumers:

- Stay in contact with lenders and try to work out a plan with them first before enlisting outside help.
- Always investigate/research the company first through the BBB. BBB Reliability Reports on debt negotiation, consolidation, and elimination companies are available online for free at www.bbb.org.
- Start with a financial credit counseling service. Credit counseling services are often non-profit and offer guidance for a small fee, or even for free.
- Beware of offers that sound too good to be true. There is no easy fix for reducing debt, and any company that makes huge claims and guarantees probably can't deliver.

The economy continues to wallow in a persistent case of stagnation, and unemployment is still rising. Against such a bleak economic climate, complaints against debt consolidation and negotiation companies are rising too, as borrowers get squeezed.

Debt consolidation companies claim to consolidate multiple debts into a single obligation, enabling the borrower to make a single, lower monthly payment to the debt consolidation company, which is responsible for paying various lenders on the borrower's behalf. The purpose of debt consolidation is to make bill-paying more manageable. However, the excessive fees and interest rates charged by many debt consolidation companies often drive consumers even further into debt.

When mounting bills threaten to derail your household finances, it's easy to feel desperate, fearful, and anxious and turn to any debt consolidation company that promises relief.

Beware of any debt consolidation company that sounds too good to be true.

Debt consolidation companies often exaggerate claims of what they can do, such as promising to cut your debt in half or remove negative records from your credit report. Other "red flags" include companies that demand high up-front fees, withhold information about their services until you provide your personal financial information, skip discussions of money management techniques or budgeting, or do not spend any time reviewing your particular situation.

How can you protect yourself from unscrupulous companies that routinely hatch debt consolidation scams to separate you from your money?

Before turning to a debt consolidation company, talk with your lenders to try to create a workable debt repayment plan. Be candid about your circumstances, but stay calm and be prepared to state the facts. Many lenders will be willing to talk to you because they realize that getting a portion of their debt repaid is better than getting nothing at all, which could happen if you declare bankruptcy.

Don't be swayed by claims of non-profit status by a debt consolidation company. Such claims have no guarantee that their services are on the up-and-up. If you do decide you need the help of a debt consolidation company, run a check on the company with the BBB. Companies that are BBB accredited meet the BBB's standards, although the BBB doesn't evaluate or endorse accredited businesses.

In addition to talking to your lenders and checking with the BBB, here are some other ways to protect yourself from debt consolidation scams:

- Research the company online: Look up the company's website and reviews from previous customers. Check if there are any complaints or negative feedback from people who have used their services before.

- Ask for references: A reputable debt consolidation company should be able to provide you with references from satisfied customers who have successfully paid off their debts through their services.

- Read the fine print: Before signing any agreements or contracts, make sure you read the terms and conditions carefully. Be wary of any company that rushes you into signing anything without giving you time to review it.

- Avoid companies that ask for upfront fees: Legitimate debt consolidation companies will not ask for payment upfront. Instead, they will take a percentage of the debt they are able to negotiate on your behalf.
- Don't give out personal information: Be cautious of any company that asks for your personal financial information before explaining their services or offering a quote.

By taking these steps, you can help protect yourself from unscrupulous debt consolidation companies and make a more informed decision about how to manage your debts.

Self-Help Debt Negotiation Vs Debt Settlement Company

Regardless of your financial situation, you can use debt settlement to manage your debts. You have the option to negotiate debt settlement by yourself or enlist the help of a debt settlement company.

If you are confident in your negotiating skills, you can negotiate with your creditors to settle your debt for a fraction of what you owe. If your creditors are not receptive to this kind of negotiation, you can persuade them to reduce your interest rate, waive past interest charges, or extend your repayment period.

In many cases, you may not need the services of a professional debt arbitrator, but having someone who knows what they are doing can be beneficial. However, regardless of whether you choose to hire a debt negotiator, it is essential to have debt negotiation skills before approaching your creditors. Interestingly, you already possess these skills because nobody understands your financial situation better than you.

Most people are afraid to talk to their creditors because they don't understand the language of the industry. However, it's not the "language" you need to know, but rather a belief in yourself. Regardless of which debt negotiation method you choose, keep in mind two things: a debt negotiator will only convey what you can tell the creditor yourself, and the creditor has the right to reject any plan the negotiator presents. By negotiating with your creditors directly, you can save money and use those funds to pay off your debts.

Self-help debt negotiation should be your first step in resolving your unsettled debts. If you have unsettled debts that you want to settle, you can negotiate with your creditors yourself. In this case, both parties are interested in finding a solution that allows you to pay a portion or all of the debt over a specified period of time. This type of negotiation enables you to make affordable payments and pay off your debt while also satisfying your creditors.

Steps to doing Self-Help Debt Negotiation:

If you face a pushy creditor that has not offered debt negotiation, you can do it yourself. Simply call up and firmly tell the creditor what you are or are not willing to do. Tell them that you want to satisfy the debt, but you cannot afford their payments, so you need to make smaller payments over a longer period of time. You can talk down your creditors so that you can pay a portion of the debt. If the creditor does not seem open to this sort of debt negotiation, you may want to try to talk them into lowering the interest rate, doing away with past interest charges, or even allowing you to repay your debt over a longer period of time. You may also tell the creditor you are willing to pay up as long as they eliminate any interest that has been charged to the account. In some situations, this is thousands of dollars, which makes the debt repayment much more doable.

The idea when dealing with a creditor during debt negotiation is to hold your ground without being rude. You should be reasonable and not only look at the situation from your point of view but also from the creditor's point of view. Usually, if you have an acceptable debt negotiation solution, the creditor will jump at it, and everyone will be happy.

Five Revised Steps for Self-Help Debt Negotiation:

1. Prepare and Research - Before you start the negotiation process, take some time to prepare yourself. You should gather all relevant information about your debts, including the total amount you owe, the interest rates, and the due dates. It's also essential to have a clear understanding of your finances and your ability to pay back the debts. Research different strategies for debt negotiation and identify the ones that would work best for your situation.

2. Contact the Creditor - Once you are ready to negotiate, contact your creditor and explain your situation. Be honest about your financial difficulties and why you are unable to make the full payments. Ask the creditor if they can work with you to come up with a payment plan that is more manageable for you. Remember to be polite and professional during the conversation.

3. Propose a Payment Plan - If the creditor is willing to work with you, propose a payment plan that you believe you can manage. This could include smaller monthly payments, a longer repayment period, or a reduced interest rate. Be specific about the terms of the plan, including the amount you will pay and the length of time it will take to pay off the debt.

4. Negotiate - The creditor may not accept your initial proposal, so be prepared to negotiate. Listen to their concerns and try to find a compromise that works for both of you. You may need to make some adjustments to your payment plan, so be flexible and open-minded.

5. Get Everything in Writing - Once you have reached an agreement with your creditor, make sure to get everything in writing. This includes the terms of the payment plan, the amount you will pay, and the due dates. Keep a copy of this agreement for your records, and make sure to stick to the payment plan.

Does Self Help Debt Negotiation Work?

Self-help debt negotiation works because it allows you to repay what you owe without going broke, while also ensuring that the creditor receives the money owed to them. It's a straightforward method that can repair your credit and get your buying power approved by top officials of the creditor. During the negotiation process, be firm and don't let the creditor make you feel guilty.

Approach the negotiation with a favorable offer and you may be able to stop receiving annoying phone calls and letters in the mail from the creditor or collector. Don't be afraid to attempt self-help negotiation; it can work as long as you don't back down.

Debt settlement is a stressful task for anyone, but it can be less daunting if you work with your creditors to find positive solutions. To negotiate debt settlements successfully, there are certain guidelines that you need to follow. This approach can help you control your financial situation before it's too late.

Communication with your creditors is the first step. Don't avoid their phone calls or any other attempts to reach you; this only compounds the problem. Even if you are not quite ready to sit down and negotiate your debt, let them know that it's your intention to do so. When a creditor calls, emails, or sends you a notice in the mail, be honest and let them know that you would like to negotiate your debts with them. Ask if you can make an appointment to discuss it. Most creditors will appreciate your effort to pay what you owe, and will be more than happy to sit down with you to figure out a way forward.

Before the meeting, do some research on your rights and on what creditors can and can't do to get you to pay what you owe. Many times aggressive debt collectors will try to convince you that you are facing certain unpleasant consequences. Being well-informed can help you when it comes time for negotiation.

Steps to Negotiating a Debt Settlement

To successfully negotiate a debt settlement, there are certain steps you can follow:

- Know your account balance: The first step is to understand your exact account balance. Find out how much of this balance is interest charges and how much are actual charges to the account. This knowledge can help you think about what you will need to say and do when you call your creditor.

- Be prepared for refusal: You can expect that the creditor may tell you they never enter into debt negotiations. If you get refusal answers, then you will want to ask for a supervisor. If they still decline your negotiation offers, you can write a letter stating that you attempted to negotiate and that you can't afford to pay under the existing conditions.

- Wait for a call back: At this step, wait for a call back from the creditor. While waiting, don't allow yourself to feel bad about your debt but learn how your creditors look at your situation.

- Find a fair offer: If you have a decent debt negotiation offer, there is a chance that your creditors will jump at it and everyone will be happy. It is important that you find an offer that is fair and agreeable to both parties.

- Hold your ground: Your debt settlement objective is to hold your ground and ensure that the terms are agreeable to you and that you are not pressured into anything. You shouldn't accept the new terms that you feel are not acceptable to you. By being firm and persistent, you can negotiate a debt settlement that works for both you and your creditor.

A Word Regarding Debt Settlement

The very first thing that must be understood is that if the original creditor sold or assigned your debt to a collection agency, then the collection agency is the only one you can talk to, so forget about running back to the original creditor because it's too late.

Secondly, before you read anything else, it is important to be clear about what is meant by the term "collection agency." It basically refers to one of three things:

1. A company that has been assigned a debt for collection
2. A company that has purchased a debt for collection
3. A lawyer who has been hired to collect a debt

The third most important thing to be clear about is which kinds of debts can you settle. These include:

- Medical bills
- Credit cards
- Personal loans
- Department store cards
- Student loans
- Bounced checks

What all of the above have in common is that they are all unsecured debts, which means that the amount owing can be negotiated. However, auto loans or mortgages are secured debts, and the lender has no reason to negotiate since they have the right to repossess them.

Assuming that the person who contacted you is a debt collector and represents a collection agency and that the debt is an unsecured one, let's look at two more things that must be verified before you even think of settling the debt.

It is important to validate the debt before settling it, which means ensuring that the company or person requesting payment is authorized to collect the debt and that the amount requested is correct. It is also important to determine if the debt is outside of the statute of limitations. If it is, you have the right to tell the debt collector to stop contacting you. However, it is important to note that just because a debt has been removed from your credit report does not mean that you no longer owe the money. Bad debts and related comments must be removed from your credit report after seven years by law, but this law only applies to credit agencies and should not be confused with the statute of limitations on debts. It is important to check the laws in your state or province to ensure you are informed.

Here are some revised Dos and Don'ts for negotiating a debt settlement:

DOs:
1. Try to handle all correspondence by mail to create a paper trail. Use registered mail and keep a copy of everything.
2. If you have to speak on the phone, make a note of the date, time, and the person you spoke to, and record the call if possible while following your local laws.
3. Believe that the agency will accept less than they say they will.
4. Stay calm and remember that the collection agency wants to strike a deal. Time is on your side, and the longer you wait, the less you may have to pay.
5. Find an offer that is fair and agreeable to both parties.
6. Validate the debt to ensure that the company or person requesting payment is authorized to collect the debt, and the amount requested is correct.

DON'Ts:
1. Don't say that you need to settle the debt, as this could create a sense of urgency that could lead to pressure to pay a higher or full amount.
2. Don't accept their first or even second offer.
3. Don't feel bad about your debt, but learn how your creditors look at your situation.
4. Don't allow yourself to be pressured into anything. Your debt settlement objective is to hold your ground and ensure that the terms are agreeable to you.
5. Don't forget that a debt collection agency does have the right to take you to court, but it is a long process that costs money and doesn't guarantee results. Keep your cool and be aware that the collection agency needs the permission of the creditor, as they do not own the debt.

So How Much Should You Offer?

When dealing with a debt collection agency, it's important to keep in mind that they typically purchase debts from original creditors for a fraction of the original amount owed. The amount they pay depends on several factors, such as the age of the debt, the type of debt, and the likelihood of being able to collect on it.

For example, if the debt is relatively recent and the agency purchased it from the original creditor, they may have paid around 5-7% of the original amount owed. However, if the debt is old and has been sold several times, the agency may have paid as little as 1% of the original amount.

Knowing this information can help you in negotiating a settlement with the debt collection agency. As a general rule, it's often best to start by offering them around 20% of the original amount owed. This amount is still likely to be profitable for the agency, but it's also low enough that it may be attractive to them to accept the offer rather than continuing to pursue the debt.

Of course, the exact amount you offer will depend on the specific circumstances of your situation, including the age and type of debt, the collection agency you're dealing with, and your own financial situation. It's important to approach negotiations with a clear understanding of your own financial limitations and to be prepared to negotiate until you reach an agreement that you're comfortable with.

Debt collection agencies may also add on extra fees or charges, which are sometimes called padding. These charges may not be directly related to the debt itself, but rather fees for their own services or administrative costs. It's important to carefully review any correspondence from the agency and make sure that the amount they are asking for is justified and accurate. If you suspect that the agency is adding on extra fees or charges that are not allowed by law or not related to the debt, then you have the right to dispute those charges and ask for proof of the debt and any additional charges. Be sure to keep records of any correspondence and receipts related to the debt and payments made.

Debt Negotiations

Don't be afraid to negotiate. Times are tough, and debt collectors are willing to accept any payments they can get. There is a good chance that you can negotiate a deal to pay less than the full amount owed. Start by offering 10% to 15% of the balance they say you owe. Then, settle for a figure around 30% to 50%. Before you pay, make sure to get the details of the deal in writing. Once you have received written confirmation of the agreement, you can proceed to make your payment. Ensure to pay with a cashier's check instead of a personal check. Under no circumstances should you provide debt collectors with access to your bank account information.

Another negotiation strategy is to offer a payment-for-deletion deal to a debt collector. You agree to pay the full amount owed, and the debt collector agrees to remove the collection account from your credit report. The debt collector would then contact the credit bureau directly to remove the debt. If you are fortunate enough to get a debt collector to agree to a pay-for-deletion deal, make sure to get it in writing in advance.

A payment-for-deletion deal is one strategy for coping with an accurate bill that was lost or forgotten but is now in collection. If the original creditor has placed your account with the credit bureau, they too will be open to this strategy.

Debt negotiation or debt settlement is the process of striking a deal with your creditors so that you can pay a reduced portion of the outstanding balance to satisfy your debt or to extend the repayment period. All parties are interested in debt settlement because it allows you to pay a portion of the debt or all of the debts over a specified period of time. This negotiation enables you to make affordable payments and get some or all of the money to the creditor to satisfy your debt. In some cases, creditors may accept a smaller amount rather than receiving nothing.

Creditors accept debt settlement for various reasons. Here are some of the essential ones:

- Getting something is better than nothing. From the creditor's point of view, it is better to negotiate than force you into bankruptcy, as they will receive nothing if bankruptcy is allowed. By negotiating the debt, the creditor will receive a percentage of what is owed. They also will not have to spend more resources trying to collect the debt. For example, if you offered to pay the creditor $500 on a balance of $1500, and the account was placed with a collection agency, the creditor would lose 25% of the $500 if it came from the agency. However, paying the creditor directly would prevent the creditor from losing that 25%.

- Creditors view debt settlement as a cost of doing business. For instance, credit card companies understand that a certain percentage of money owed to them will be written off. The offset for these write-offs is charging a higher interest rate to many customer debtors. In their business plan, they have accounted for negotiated debt reduction. Using credit card companies as an example, the higher interest rates to cover write-offs allows for more profit from those paying debtors.

Most creditors negotiate debts for the same reason. Getting a debt settled is a means to get some money out of the debtor. Clearing the books of bad or underperforming debts keeps the business clean and is less costly in the long run.

The Down and Dirty:

A Quick Look at How Debt Collection Agencies Operate

The Collector's Advantage

Let's delve into the world of debt collectors. Firstly, not everyone can become a collector. It takes a specific personality to be successful in this field, as the primary goal is to collect money, which requires remaining emotionless. The reason why the bill cannot be paid does not matter; the debtor used the services or money and did not pay. Therefore, you owe the money, and as a collector, I am not there to listen to your problems, but to collect the money you owe.

If you can purchase cigarettes, beer, or go out to a nightclub, you can pay your debt. There is no logical reason why you cannot pay. Besides, I already know your living situation by looking at your file. I know if you own your home or pay rent, and I know how much your mortgage or rent is. I know if you own your car or if you are making payments and how much you are paying. I also know where you bank and what type of accounts you have.

I know if you are employed and who your employer is and how long you have worked there. I even know how long you have lived at your current address. In fact, I know if you have had trouble paying any of your accounts before and if you have any previous credit history, liens, garnishments, judgments, etc. All of this information is available to me before I make the call. It provides me with a "picture" of what "type" of debtor you are. The information is like a "profile" of you.

You may ask how all of this information is possible. That's not a mystery. When you applied for a credit card, personal loan, car loan, etc., the creditor ran a credit report. Prior to that, the creditor asked you to fill out a loan application. Remember when I stated earlier that all pertinent information was included in the file when the creditor sent it to the collection agency? Well, that information came along with it. As a collector, I review the information before making the call. It enables me to formulate my conversation based on the information I already know about you. If your credit report shows that you've had trouble before, then you know the system, and I'll converse accordingly. If you are someone who struggles, I'll adjust. The bottom line is, I have the advantage.

Some may argue that this is too much information for a collection agency to have. I may agree, but remember the fine print at the bottom of or included in a paragraph in which the creditor stated they could "share" information with third parties. As the collection agency is a third party assigned by the creditor to collect money owed to them, they can contract the agency out, thus providing them with information about you. In essence, the collector has "profiled" you into his approach when talking to you, but the one constant that remains the same and always will be, as long as there is bad debt, is intimidation.

Debt collectors have a job to do, and many collectors perform this distasteful duty in a professional manner. Debt collectors who act professionally usually do so because they received training on how to collect debts without violating any laws or consumer protection guidelines. To stay focused on their collection efforts and not violate those laws or guidelines, many collection agencies and independent bill collectors use a generic script. Keep in mind that there is no formal training to become a debt collector. All that is needed is a desire to convince someone to pay a debt. It is a good idea for the agency to supply the debt collector with a script to avoid lawsuits for violations. Being aware of what a typical script looks like can help you prepare answers to a debt collector's questions ahead of time

An Inside Look - The Collection Agency

Like any other business, collection agencies compete for business. Just about any company that has a service or sells a product Is a potential client. The sales pitch to obtain the business is based on how good the agency is at collecting past due accounts. The creditor usually will pass the account on after a 120 day period or after they have tried to collect and are unsuccessful. Most creditors believe that the agency will have better results because of the myth that debt collection agencies are more intimidating. Besides, paying the standard agency fee of 25% of what they collect is better than nothing.

If the creditor decides to use a debt collection agency, they will gather all of their past due accounts, most often in the thousands at a time and pass them on to the agency. Along with those accounts is any pertinent information such as the contract, applications, original credit check etc. Sometimes the creditor will also provide notes that they have taken when they did contact the debtor which becomes part of the file. This process is written out in the contract between the creditor and the debt collection agency. The contract will also states what the agency collecting fee is which can be anywhere between 25 to 50%.

Part of that agreement is that the agency will provide a status report to the creditor every 30 days that shows activity on each account the creditor has assigned to the agency along with a remittance of monies collected. The creditor provides an accounting of each balance due that is to be collected. Also, the creditor will stipulate how long the agency has to collect on the accounts; it could be 3 months, 6 months, or longer.

Once the accounts are received by the agency, they are put into the system and distributed among the collectors. Prior to any collection activity beginning, a "DUN" letter (demand for payment), is sent to the last known address as provided by the creditor.

The "DUN" letter must state the name of the agency, the name of the creditor, and the amount owed. This information is what the creditor gave to the agency and is what is on the actual account. The account has other information such as the last date the creditor received a payment, the interest amount, and balance due. At this point, the creditor has no further contact with the debtor as they have turned the account over to the agency. If you should call the creditor, they will respond to your call stating that they no longer have the account as it was turned over to collections.

Usually the creditor has sent a notice advising the debtor that the account will be placed with an agency within a length of time and advise that in order to prevent that action, payment to cover the arrears and bring the account current is required.

The creditor does have a listing of accounts in their systems that were turned over to the agency, but they do not have the actual account itself. After a short period of time, usually 10 days/the collection agency begins its collection activity on the accounts that it obtained from the creditor.

Up to this point, the reader has a foundation of the debt from the creditor to the debt collection agency. There is more but this book is not about the business or the inner workings of a collection agency. It is about dealing with bad debt collectors and the agencies in general.

It is at this moment, that the reader will discover how the debt industry bends and in some cases, violates the Consumer Protection guidelines.

Junk Debt Buyers

A junk debt buyer is a company that buys defaulted credit accounts. They buy this debt for pennies on the dollar and then try to collect on the "junk" debt.

"Junk" debt gets its name in the following manner. "John Doe" defaults on a credit card account. The original creditor attempts to collect what is owed from "John Doe". If the original creditor fails, they charge off the debt (charge off is an accounting term that means "uncollectible debt", it does not mean that you no longer owe the debt). After the charge off, the defaulted account is placed with other defaulted accounts into a portfolio, and the portfolio is sold to the highest bidder, often a junk debt buyer.

People often say "I didn't agree to that" or "They can't sue me because I did not agree to the sale," but your agreement is not necessary when it comes to the purchase or sale of a defaulted credit account.

Once you default on an account, the original creditor obtains the right to sue you for the balance owed. This is called a "legal interest". Any legal interest can be sold to anyone for any price, and the individual has nothing to say about the transaction.

The junk debt buyer then attempts to collect on the debt. This usually starts with a phone call or letter, but it can quickly escalate into the filing of a lawsuit. Believe it or not, a lawsuit from a junk debt buyer is to your benefit. In my experience, I have found that junk debt buyers often do not acquire all of the necessary documentation that is needed to prevail in a court of law against debtors (individuals who owe money or who have defaulted on credit accounts). The typical package that a junk debt buyer acquires consists of the debtor's name, address, telephone number, account number, charge off date, and amount allegedly owed. Many other documents and pieces of evidence are needed to prevail in a court of law.

Here is a quick look at how bad debt is bought and sold in the United States:

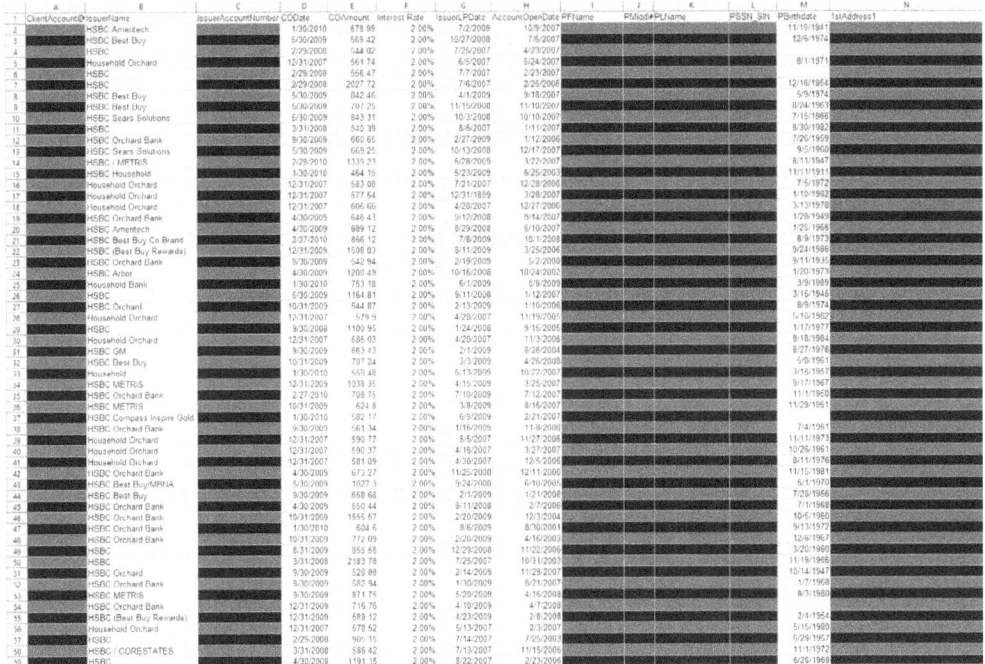

Due to Privacy Reasons, many of the personal information must be blanked out.

This example is from a portfolio that included 1,209 other delinquent accounts. These Excel sheets list everything from the amount owed, interest rate, and last payment date. However, it also lists personal information such as the social security number, address, city and state, current and previous employment, home and work phone numbers, and contact information for friends and family.

Typically, this single document is all that junk debt buyers purchase from each other to attempt to collect on your debt. However, many times these sales do not include the original contract, signatures, or application forms. Therefore, it is crucial to demand that debt collection companies validate your debt. More often than not, they cannot produce a single document in their defense.

In Canada, the process is very similar, although the original creditors hold onto delinquent accounts until the statute of limitations has passed (which will be addressed later in this book), after which the debt is eventually sold to junk debt buyers. These types of documents contain the same information regardless of the type of debt owed, whether it be credit card debt, payday loans, bad checks, furniture financing debt, or cellphone debt. Chances are, your name and information are on one or more of these lists.

EDUCATE YOURSELF,
Know the laws, know your rights.

Debt Collection Laws

For many people, having their debt turned over to a collection agency is an absolute worst-case scenario. These debt collection agencies have earned a reputation for being persistent, difficult to work with and almost impossible to shake.

Although most debt collection agencies work within the professional and ethical bounds of the industry, there have been numerous cases of harassment and fraud reported in the industry to warrant stricter laws.

And while broader government oversight has achieved much to reign in collection practices across North America, it's important for you to understand the debt collection laws agents must follow, your rights when dealing with a collection agent what you can do when either of these are being violated.

The Fair Debt Collection Practices Act (FDCPA) is a federal law in the United States that regulates the behavior of debt collectors. It prohibits debt collectors from engaging in unfair, deceptive, or abusive practices when attempting to collect a debt. Some of the key provisions of the FDCPA include restrictions on when and where debt collectors can contact you, prohibitions on threats of violence or harm, and requirements to provide certain information about the debt.

In Canada, the rules and regulations governing debt collection practices vary by province, but they all aim to protect consumers from abusive or harassing practices. For example, in Ontario, the Collection and Debt Settlement Services Act (CDSSA) governs the activities of debt collectors and debt settlement companies. It requires that collectors be licensed and follow strict rules for contacting debtors, and it prohibits them from engaging in certain types of behavior, such as making false or misleading statements or threatening legal action that they cannot take.

If you feel that a debt collector is violating the law or engaging in abusive or harassing behavior, there are steps you can take to protect yourself. You can request that the collector stop contacting you, or you can file a complaint with the appropriate regulatory agency. In some cases, you may even be able to sue the debt collector for damages if they have violated your rights under the law.

It's important to understand your rights and the laws governing debt collection practices, so that you can protect yourself and ensure that debt collectors are treating you fairly and within the bounds of the law.

Collection Agency Rules

Because debt collection is state or provincially regulated, debt collectors must obtain a license in each state or province they operate in and conduct themselves according to federal and state/provincial debt collection laws and principles of conduct.

Across North America, there are explicit guidelines governing what debt collectors can (and cannot) do to recover a debt. However, the following rules apply universally under federal law:

Contact:

- Debt collectors must make a reasonable attempt to notify a debtor in writing that a creditor has turned their account over to a collection agency.
- Debt collectors may contact a debtor Monday: Saturday between 7:00 a.m. and 9:00 p.m. and on Sundays between 1:00 p.m. and 5:00 p.m.
- Debt collectors may contact friends, family, neighbors, or employers, but only to request a debtor's telephone number and current mailing address.
- Debt collectors may not contact debtors on statutory holidays.
- Debt collectors may not disclose personal or financial information to friends, family, neighbors, or employers nor may they suggest those individuals pay the outstanding debt if they have not co-signed for them.

Conduct:

- Debt collectors must identify themselves as such at the outset of any communication.
- Debt collectors must conduct themselves ethically, honestly, and professionally.
- Debt collectors may not use threatening, intimidating, or abusive language.
- Debt collectors may not apply excessive or unreasonable pressure to repay the debt.

Fees and Legal Action:

- Debt collectors may not recommend legal or court action without first informing you.
- Debt collectors may not add any collection-related costs to the outstanding debt other than legal fees and fees for insufficient funds from payment.

You may be wondering why you've been receiving calls at all hours of the day or why the agent was rude, abusive, and threatening legal action. The reason for this is because there is a difference between a debt collection agency working on behalf of the creditor and junk debt buyers that own the debt. The laws in the United States and Canada mostly apply to collection agencies working on behalf of the original creditor, and junk debt buyers who own the debt have no such laws to follow. The only law that applies to all debt is the statute of limitations.

Consumer's Rights

As a consumer, you have certain rights when it comes to debt collection. Firstly, you have the right to dispute any debt that a collection agency claims you owe to a creditor. Additionally, you have the right to hire a lawyer to handle any contact with collection agencies. Once a lawyer is appointed, collection agencies are required to stop contacting you directly and can only communicate with your attorney.

You also have the right to receive written notice of any debt owed and a notice of potential legal action before any further action is taken by the collection agency. Collection agencies are prohibited from using abusive or threatening language or engaging in any behavior intended to intimidate you. They should not contact you more than three times within a seven-day period unless it is through mail.

When to file a complaint

When considering filing a complaint against a collection agency, it's important to understand your rights and when they have been violated. If you're unsure about your rights or suspect that they have been violated, you can contact your local consumer protection agency or bureau for guidance. You can typically reach them by phone, email, mail, or fax.

It's important to note that filing a complaint with a consumer protection agency or bureau does not release you from your obligation to pay the debt you owe, regardless of the length of time it has been outstanding or the conduct of the collection agency. Filing a complaint is a way to hold the collection agency accountable for their actions and to seek resolution to any violations of your rights.

The statutes of limitations set a time limit for when a creditor or collection agency can legally pursue legal action to collect a debt. The purpose of these limitations is to ensure that due process is expedited, evidence is preserved, and equity and fairness are maintained for both the debtor and the creditor. For debt collection, statutes of limitations protect debtors from facing civil lawsuits and court judgments for unpaid debts that have been in default for an extended period of time.

Statute of Limitations

Statutes of limitations are laws that dictate how long creditors or collection agencies have to file a lawsuit against a debtor for an outstanding debt. The time-frame varies depending on the state or province, and the type of debt in question. In most cases, the clock starts ticking from the date of the last payment or activity on the account.

The primary purpose of statutes of limitations is to ensure that legal action is taken within a reasonable amount of time after the debt goes into default. This helps to ensure that evidence is preserved, and that the defendant has a fair opportunity to defend themselves. Additionally, statutes of limitations help to prevent creditors and collection agencies from endlessly pursuing debtors for money they may no longer be able to pay, which can cause undue stress and financial hardship.

If a debt collector or creditor attempts to sue a debtor after the statute of limitations has expired, the debtor can use the statute of limitations as a defense in court. If successful, the court will dismiss the case, and the debtor will not be required to pay the debt. However, it's important to note that even if the statute of limitations has expired, the debt itself does not disappear. The creditor or collection agency may still attempt to collect on the debt through other means, such as phone calls or letters, but they cannot file a lawsuit to collect the debt.

In Canada

the statute of limitations for legal action in debt collection is typically six years from the time the debtor has defaulted on the debt. It's important to note that the time-frame starts from the very last payment made to the creditor. However, this time-frame resets whenever the debtor makes a payment towards or otherwise formally acknowledges the debt in question. Each province and territory has its own statutes of limitations that vary from two to six years. For example, Alberta has a statute of limitations of two years, while Quebec has a three-year statute of limitations.

It's important to note that the statute of limitations only means that the collector or creditor cannot legally obtain payment for the debt. Remedies such as judgments, garnishments, and liens are not allowed. However, the debt will still show on the debtor's credit report as "unpaid" and can remain there for at least six years. To remove the debt, the debtor can offer a settlement amount to the collector or creditor, and they will have to remove it. If they do not, the debtor can write to the credit bureau and provide them with proof of the settlement, and they will remove it.

Each province and territory also has their own statutes of limitations, which are as follows:

B.C.: Six years
Alberta: Two years*
Saskatchewan: Two years
Manitoba: Six years
Ontario: Two years**
Quebec: Three years
New Brunswick: Six years
Nova Scotia: Six years
P.E.I.: Six years
Newfoundland and Labrador: Two years
Yukon: Six years
Northwest Territories: Six years
Nunavut: Six years

*In the event of a court judgment prior to the original statute of limitations expiring, the creditor has 10 years to collect.
**This statue of limitation resets whenever a debtor acknowledges or makes a payment toward their outstanding debt within that two-year window.

NOTE: This means that the collector or creditor cannot legally force you to pay the debt through legal remedies such as judgments, garnishments, or liens once the statute of limitations has expired. However, the unpaid debt will still appear on your credit report and can stay there for at least six years. To remove the debt from your credit report, you can offer a settlement amount to the collector or creditor. Once the settlement is reached, they will have to remove the debt from your credit report. If they refuse to do so, you can write to the credit bureau and provide proof of the settlement, and they will remove it.

In the United States

debts are categorized into one of four categories, and it is crucial to know which type of debt you have because the time limits for each category vary. If you are unsure about which type of debt you have, it is best to seek legal advice from an attorney.

The four categories of debt are:

- Oral Agreements: These are debts that were made based on a verbal agreement to repay the money, and there is nothing in writing.

- Written Contracts: All debts that come with a contract that was signed by you and the creditor falls into this category, even if it was written on a napkin. However, the contract must include the terms and conditions of the loan, such as the loan amount and the monthly payment. Medical debts are one kind of written contract.

- Promissory Notes: A promissory note is a written agreement to repay a debt in certain payments, at a specific interest rate, and by a certain date and time. Home loans and student loans are examples of promissory notes.

- Open-Ended Accounts: An account with a revolving balance you can repay and then borrow again is open-ended. Credit cards, in-store credit, and lines of credit are examples of open-ended accounts. If you can only borrow the money for a specific period, it is not an open-ended account.

Each state has its own statute of limitations on debt, and they vary depending on the type of debt you have. Usually, it ranges between three and six years, but it can be as high as 10 or 15 years in some states. It is crucial to find out the debt statute of limitations for your state before responding to a debt collection.

These are the statutes of limitation, measured in years, for each state:

State	Oral	Written	Promissory	Open
Alabama	6	6	6	3
Alaska	3	3	3	3
Arizona	3	6	6	3
Arkansas	3	5	3	3
California	2	4	4	4
Colorado	6	6	6	6
Connecticut	3	6	6	3
Delaware	3	3	3	4
Florida	4	5	5	4
Georgia	4	6	6	6
Hawaii	6	6	6	6
Idaho	4	5	5	5
Illinois	5	10	10	5

State	Oral	Written	Promissory	Open
Indiana	6	6	10	6
Iowa	5	10	5	5
Kansas	3	5	5	3
Kentucky	5	10	15	5
Louisiana	10	10	10	3
Maine	6	6	6	6
Maryland	3	3	6	3
Massachusetts	6	6	6	6
Michigan	6	6	6	6
Minnesota	6	6	6	6
Mississippi	3	3	3	3
Missouri	5	10	10	5
Montana	5	8	8	5
Nebraska	4	5	5	4
Nevada	4	6	3	4
New Hampshire	3	3	6	3
New Jersey	6	6	6	6
New Mexico	4	6	6	4
New York	6	6	6	6
North Carolina	3	3	5	3
North Dakota	6	6	6	6
Ohio	6	8	15	6
Oklahoma	3	5	5	3
Oregon	6	6	6	6
Pennsylvania	4	4	4	4
Rhode Island	10	10	10	10
South Carolina	3	3	3	3
South Dakota	6	6	6	6
Tennessee	6	6	6	6
Texas	4	4	4	4
Utah	4	6	6	4
Vermont	6	6	5	3
Virginia	3	5	6	3
Washington	3	6	6	3
West Virginia	5	10	6	5
Wisconsin	6	6	10	6
Wyoming	8	10	10	8

Your Credit Report and YOU!

Your Credit Report and YOU!

North America has two major credit bureaus, Equifax and TransUnion, which collect, analyze, and report information about you and your financial history. Before issuing new or additional debt, creditors will generally purchase a credit report from one or both of these bureaus to determine your creditworthiness.

Your credit report includes details obtained from several sources, including credit applications, creditor records, and public records. These details can include your name, address, employer details, any bankruptcies, court judgments, foreclosures or payment agreements, account numbers, outstanding balances of current debts, and any closed, inactive or defaulted credit accounts within the past six years. Additionally, your credit report features a nine-point rating reflecting your payment history for each of the above debts.

Consumers have the right to know the information documented in their credit report, as well as its source. The details and ratings within their credit report can have significant implications for their ability to secure new credit, including the credit limits and interest rates they qualify for, the down payments required, and whether they require a co-signer. Consistently late payments, collections action, and bad debt all significantly reduce a consumer's ability to obtain new credit.

It's important to note that creditors, debt collectors, and other third parties may not view a consumer's credit report without their express written consent, which generally comes in the form of a signed waiver. In the case of debt collectors acting on behalf of a creditor which has obtained consent, permission also extends to them within the scope of that purpose.

Getting your Credit Report

The first step to improving your financial standing and removing bad debt is to obtain your credit report from both Equifax and TransUnion, the two major credit bureaus in North America. It's important to get reports from both bureaus as they often manage and rate debt differently. Even though they are legally required to have identical information on you, they may present different information and not provide a complete picture of your credit situation.

Don't hesitate to obtain your credit reports, even if it causes anxiety or stress. Knowing which creditors or debt collectors are reporting and the amounts they claim you owe will enable you to tackle each item accurately. All credit reports list the creditor's or debt collector's contact information and account numbers. If you find any discrepancies in your report, take the necessary steps to correct them.

You can obtain your credit report in various ways, depending on how urgently you need it. You can get it immediately for a fee or request a free report once a year by mail, fax, or telephone. Order a copy of your credit report from both Equifax and TransUnion, as each bureau may have different information about your credit usage history. It's important to note that ordering your own credit report won't affect your credit score.

Order by mail or fax

- Make your request in writing using the forms provided by Equifax and TransUnion on their websites.
- Provide copies of two pieces of acceptable identification, such as a driver's license or passport

Order by telephone

Call the credit bureau and follow the instructions

Equifax
Canada   Tel: 1-800-465-7166
USA   Tel: 1-800-685-1111

TransUnion
Canada   Tel: 1-800-663-9980 (except Quebec)
Tel: 1-877-713-3393 (Quebec residents)
USA   Tel: 1-800-888-4213

- Confirm your identity by answering a series of personal and financial questions
- You may also need to provide your Social Insurance Number and/or a credit card number to confirm your identity

Get your credit report online

If you want to get your credit report online and instantaneously then there will be a fee (usually around 25$). The advantage here is that there is an option to see your credit score, and, you can see It Instantly. TransUnion allows you to order your credit report online once a month for free.

You may also sign up for free credit reporting using companies such has Borrowell.com or Creditkarma.com. These websites will give you a majority of the information needed to be informed, but may lack the nitty gritty of the formulas that make up your score.

How to read your credit report.

The 2 major credit bureaus operate with a credit score range between 300 and 900. the lower your score, the less likely you are to be approved for a credit card or loan. If you do manage to qualify for a credit card or loan despite having a low score, the interest rate you will receive will likely be very high.

Conversely, the higher your credit score, the more likely you are to be approved for a credit card or loan, and the lower the interest rate will likely be.

Your credit score goes up and down based on the information in your report. For example: making regular payments, on time, will gradually make your score rise, but missing payments will make it drop. And holding a large balance close to your credit limit month after month will also make it drop.

Excellent (741-900)

Consumers with excellent credit will likely have no or very few late payments in their credit report, will regularly pay off their balances in full, and will have a low credit utilization across all their lines of credit.

Good (690-740)

Consumers with a credit score in this range still enjoy some of the best financial products and interest rates available. This credit score means you are generally financially responsible: consumers who sit in this credit score range make most of their payments on time with only the occasional late payment on rare occasions.

Fair/Average (660-689)

consumers still have a lot of credit options at the 'average' credit score evaluation, but borrowers on the lower end of this range will certainly experience higher interest rates from lenders. Those on the mid to lower end probably have been late on their payments multiple times to more than one lender and may have defaulted on a loan at some point.

Below Average (575-659)

consumers with below average credit will face higher interest rates for the lines of credit they are approved for. Consumers at this level are likely to have 1 or more defaults on loans or have items currently in collections.

Poor (300-574)

If you're in this credit score range, you unfortunately have a significantly damaged credit history. Perhaps you have defaulted on multiple loans, your debt is very close to your credit limit, or you have declared bankruptcy, which stays on your credit report for at least seven years. In this range it is near impossible to apply for new loans.

Some credit bureaus report a rating of every item on your credit history individually and the rating ranges from 1 to 9, where a rating of 1 shows that all payments are on time, and a rating of 9 means that bills are never paid or a consumer proposal has been submitted to the lender.

Sometimes you will see a letter before the number (e.g. I3). You can have one of three letters before each number: **I, O, R,** and they mean the following:

- **I**: your loan is being repaid with regular installments for a specific period of time. I is for installment.
- **O**: you have open credit, such as a line of credit or student loans. O is for open.O
- **R**: this implies revolving credit, where your payments depend on your account balance. A good example is a credit card. R is for revolving credit, and this is the most common type of credit rating.

These are the different R ratings one can have, in accordance with the North American Standard Account ratings:

- R0: Too little credit history or, credit unused.
- R1: Pays (or paid) within 30 days of payment due date or not over one payment past due.
- R2: Pays (or paid) in more than 30 days from payment due date, but not more than 60 days, or not more than two payments past due.
- R3: Pays (or paid) in more than 60 days from payment due date, but not more than 90 days, or not more than three payments past due.
- R4: Pays (or paid) in more than 90 days from payment due date, but not more than 120 days, or four payments past due.
- R5: Account is at least 120 days overdue, but is not yet rated.
- R6: This rating does not exist.
- R7: Making regular payments through a special arrangement to settle your debts.
- R8: Repossession (voluntary or involuntary return of merchandise).
- R9: Bad debt; placed for collection; moved without giving a new address or bankruptcy.

All these codes along with your credit utilization (amount you owe in comparison to your credit limit) make up your credit score. Knowing how to modify and manipulate different aspects of your credit score by knowing how they record and operate will help you clean up and raise your credit score.

FIGHT BACK!

Tip and tricks, forms and tactics

Quick Tips for Negotiating with Collection Agencies

When dealing with collection agencies, negotiating a fair settlement is essential to getting your finances back on track. Here are some tips to help you through the process:

- Find out the Statute of Limitations (SOL) on your debts. This is the time allotted by the court for debt recovery. Once this period is over, the creditor is no longer allowed to attempt debt collection.
- Check the SOL in your state or province as they vary from one to another.
- If the SOL period is still valid, inform the creditor about it and negotiate the total amount you owe.
- If the creditor doesn't agree on the negotiation, let them know that you may opt for filing bankruptcy.
- All communication and transactions should be in writing.
- Let the creditor take the initiative to ask how much they can waive off the total amount. They are more likely to ask for a negotiation amount, after which you can put forth your amount. Quote a lower amount than you actually intend to pay the lender.
- Take your time during negotiations. The more time you take, the more likely the creditor will quote a lower amount.
- Try to get the amount reduced as much as possible. In some cases, it is possible to get the amount reduced to approximately 70% of the due amount.
- Consider getting the records on your credit report corrected. Ask the lender if they can remove negative records or statements from your credit report if you pay them a portion of the due amount in a lump sum. A clear credit report is important for future financial transactions.

Questions Asked By Collectors

Earlier I brought up the issue regarding how much information the collection agency and the collectors have before they place a phone call to you. Any questions that they ask during their phone call are for two reasons. They are to validate what they already know or to gather information to ascertain your ability to pay the debt and to gather information for possible suit.

Be prepared to answer questions but think carefully and consider each question you choose to answer. Remember, you do NOT have to answer ANY questions. If you choose to answer questions, think before you answer and weigh heavily the information you may be providing a stranger.

Additionally, if you are uncomfortable answering any questions, you can politely decline and ask them to communicate with you in writing instead. It's important to know your rights and not feel pressured or intimidated during these conversations. Remember, you have the right to be treated fairly and respectfully under the law.

Here are questions you can answer:
1. Do I have your address right at (street), city and (province) and (zip code)?
2. Is this (or what) your daytime phone _____?

Note: After answering this question, inform the caller that any future calls between (hours) and on (days) are inconvenient.
- Where do you work?
- What is the address and phone number of your employer?

Note: *Collectors are allowed to call and verify employment BUT that is all. They are not allowed to discuss your information, nor are they entitled to any information about your Income or any other personal information.*

Here are questions you do **NOT** have to answer:
- Are you paid weekly or bi-weekly?
- How much is your take-home pay?
- Is your spouse working? If so, how are they paid? Amount, etc.
- Do you have other sources of income; (child support, part-time work, etc)
- Do you rent or own?
- How much per month? Is it current?
- What make, model and year of your car is?
- Where do you bank? (Checking and savings, name of bank)?
- Do you have any bank loans? How much do you owe? Are they current?
- Have you ever borrowed money form (parents, relatives, and friends) in the past? If so, how long ago? How much? Did you pay it back?

If you choose to answer any of those questions then expect the collector to put you on hold while he figures out the best suggestion for you to pay off the debt. Typically they will come back with, "If I could show you a way to pay this debt off, would you be willing to work with me?" OR "Your current balance that you owe is $3,700. I can settle this account for you if you pay $2,000.00"

Unless they suggest a payment plan that you can afford **DO NOT** agree to anything. Consider your answer carefully. Counter with a payment agreement of your own (only suggest what you can truly afford) and ask about credit reporting information. You want to keep it off your credit reports so make this part of your payment agreement if the account has not yet been reported.

In the follow pages, are 2 example conversations with debt collectors using the tips tricks and knowledge that you have learned so far. Obviously not all conversations over the phone will be exactly like this, but armed with this knowledge will shows that you are in control and you will not be taken advantage of.

Example Conversation #1 - You Believe the Debt to Be Invalid

Collector: "Hello, is John Doe there?" (Or is this John doe's wife?)

You: "Who is calling please?" (Do not let the use of your first name throw you off guard. Always confirm who you are speaking with. Under the Consumer Protection guidelines, collectors must identify themselves and their company.)

Collector: "This is Mr. Collector from ABC Collections, the collection agency representing Generic Furniture Company on your outstanding balance of $3,700. I need to know if you are able to take care of this past due bill at this time.

You: "Hold on while I turn on my audio recorder. (After turning on recorder ask the collector to repeat his or her name, company and the reason for calling.) Then say. "I do not believe I owe this debt. Send me the information on this debt according to the Consumer Protection guidelines so I may review it."

Expect the collector to use questions or statements in an attempt to get you to admit the debt is yours. Do not answer these questions, stick to the answer outlined above and insists on the collector following the Consumer Protection guidelines by sending you the proper information - stay focused.

Their script tells them to ignore your response and press on with asking you a bunch of questions. By refusing to take the "bait" you frustrate their efforts because your answer is not in their script. At this point, many collectors are unsure of what to say or do next so they resort to anger. Remain calm and be sure your audio recorder is on.

Note: Once you've verbally disputed a debt, there is only one question that you need to answer:

Collector: "Please verify your address"

You: Go ahead and provide your correct address.

If the collector doesn't ask you to confirm your address, don't expect a validation as they're not required to send you one. There may be a reason to confirm your address, but in reality, they already have it. They sent you a "DUN" letter about 10 days prior, and it never came back, so unless you've moved, the question is redundant. On the other hand, the collector may state that they will send you a letter. The letter they send will be the same "DUN" letter you've already received. That's not a validation letter. The next time the collector calls, and you request validation, they will state that they have sent one. Advise them that you are requesting they abide by the Consumer Protection guidelines and repeat your request.

The validation of debt is extremely important for many reasons that the consumer may not consider. Besides it being the correct amount, there are other serious reasons for validating. It was mentioned earlier that the creditor gathers many past due accounts to be turned over to the agency for collection. Suppose that within that time period, you sent a payment in. The account is in a pile waiting to be sent to collections, and the payment you sent does not get posted. The balance prior to it being sent to the agency was $500.00. You sent in a $100 payment to the creditor, but it was not credited to the account, which would be a balance of $400.00 if it had. You have a receipt that you paid it, and when the collector calls, you know the balance is wrong. That's just the beginning. Secondly, the collection agency has reported the account with a $500 delinquency to the credit bureau, and yet you know you made a payment and that the reported delinquent amount is wrong.

The collection agency may report a delinquent account before it is validated as true and correct, which goes against Consumer Protection guidelines. If the agency threatens to report the debt to the credit bureau but fails to provide validation, it is also a violation of these guidelines. Some collection agencies may add additional fees to the delinquent account, such as agency fees, interest fees, and service fees. However, they cannot charge interest fees that are higher than the original contractual fees set by the creditor. By requesting validation, consumers can expose any discrepancies associated with the account, including these additional fees. While consumer guidelines do not currently outline the validation issue, failure to receive validation while the collector continues to call and request payment on an incorrect or disputed debt can leave consumers without means of protecting themselves.

If a consumer does not owe the amount stated, it is unlikely that they will pay it. However, if the collector ignores the consumer's request for validation, continues to call and potentially reports the debt to the credit bureau, it becomes a problem. The current Consumer Protection guidelines need to be expanded to include a requirement that the collector sends the validation to the consumer upon request. Additionally, collection activity should cease until the same amount of time has lapsed as in the original DUN letter. It is essential that no account is entered by the collection agency until the validation has occurred. The "DUN" letter should clearly state that the consumer has the right to request validation on the debt and the period in which they may do so. If the consumer does not request validation, the agency can proceed. Validation is important, as discussed earlier, with regard to Statute of Limitations and Junk Debt Buyers (JDB).

Collectors are trained to DUN (collect or ask for payment) in the following priority:

1. Balance in full;
2. Settlement (in no more than two payments);
3. Payments over three months, usually not to exceed six months;
4. Good faith payment while you ask others for a loan (parents, friends, bank, etc.).

Since they want the full amount as quickly as possible, they will refuse just about anything you offer and try to force you to agree with their terms. Unless you're extremely good at negotiating, never negotiate terms on the phone - you'll likely lose every time.

Collection agencies, bill collectors, and junk debt buyers are trained to get payments in the following priority:

1. Auto Pay - involves withdrawals from your bank accounts via post-dated checks, automatic electronic withdrawals, or other similar methods.
2. Priority Mail
3. Certified Mail

When making payment arrangements with collectors, remember that although collectors will insist on you paying by their preferred method, there is no law compelling you to pay by any of these methods. You can pay by any method that does not provide information about your bank account to the collector.

The best method of payment is to use a money order and send it via certified mail. It is important to never pay using a post-dated check or an automatic withdrawal process because there is a risk of the check being cashed early or more funds being withdrawn than authorized, leading to returned checks and overdrawn charges.

It is also important to avoid falling into the trap of a "good faith" payment arrangement. This approach will only lead to deeper debt and more financial problems. Borrowing from one credit card to pay off another debt or going deeper in debt to borrow money is not a sensible solution. It is unlikely that a bank will loan money to someone who is already in debt, and the collector knows this, but their priority is to pressure the debtor into making a payment regardless of the consequences. It is essential to keep in mind that the collector's concern is to collect the debt, and they are not concerned about the debtor's financial situation.

Example Conversationv#2 - You Believe the Debt Might Be Valid But You Are Unsure

Collector: "Hello, is John Doe there?" (Or is this John doe's wife?)

You: "Who is calling please?" (Do not let the use of your first name throw you off guard. Always confirm who you are speaking with. Under the Consumer Protection guidelines, collectors must identify themselves and their company.)

Collector: "This is Mr. Collectors from ABC Collections, the collection agency representing Payday Loan 123 Company Due on your outstanding balance of $2,400. I need to know if you are able to take care of this past due bill at this time.

You: "Hold on while I get my audio recorder." Take your time and THINK before saying anything. Is it possible that the debt has expired? (See statute of Limitations.) If the S.O.L. has expired (or you're not sure) revert to example Conversation#1. If the S.O.L. has not expired, then ask:

You: "Are you collecting on behalf of a creditor, your employer or yourself?" Until the collector answers this question, **DO NOT** answer any other questions.

IMPORTANT: If the debt is new, the collector is probably working for the creditor. If the debt is more than 1-2 years old it's a good bet the debt was sold and this collector (or his company) purchased it. If the collector owns the debt and you do **NOT** wish to pay the debt state: (be sure your tape recorder is on beforehand.)

You: "It is my policy to never deal with debt collectors who are not representing the creditor. Give me your address so that I may send you a cease and desist letter."

The script above touches on the issue of an account being out of statute. There are three things you can do if the account is out of the Statute of Limitations;

- you can let it go and not pay it.
- you can make a payment and start the account time period all over again or,
- you can offer a settlement.

Just because the account is out-of-statute, that does not mean it will not appear on your credit report. It can remain on your credit report for years. An account out-of-statute means that the collection agency cannot use legal remedies like court actions, such as a judgment, garnishment, or liens to force you to pay. However, making a payment can restart the collection process and open the door for the agency to take you to court. Ignoring the debt will only keep it on your credit report and hurt your chances of obtaining a loan in the future.

You can offer a settlement to clear the debt, but keep in mind that Junk Debt Buyers purchase old debt for pennies on the dollar. It's reasonable to propose paying a similar amount to clear the debt. If the creditor or agency refuses your offer, you can provide the credit bureau with evidence of your offer and their refusal. They cannot force you to pay the original amount. If the debt was never validated, there's no guarantee that the amount they claim you owe is correct.

Mailing & Record Keeping Instructions

General:

It is crucial to keep copies of all correspondence when dealing with creditors, debt collectors, credit reporting agencies, and credit repair agencies. This means making copies of all letters sent and received, along with their envelopes. If a creditor, debt collector, or credit reporting or repair agency violates the law, these records can serve as evidence in court. Accurate records are also necessary if you need to hire a lawyer or file a formal complaint.

To ensure delivery and proof of receipt, it is recommended to send a fax and a certified copy via U.S. mail or Canada Post, as well as standard first-class mail with proof of mailing. By doing so, you have taken extra steps to ensure the message is received and can prove it if necessary. Here is a checklist to use when preparing and sending your letters.

Preparing Documents to Fax and Mail

Step 1: Write the letter (initial or follow-up dispute, creditor's agreement, or free credit report request, etc.). Consider handwriting your letter, but if you type it, be sure to sign it and send the original to avoid it looking like a form letter.

Step 2: Sign and date all letters in **BLACK INK**!

Step 3: Make two copies of your signed letter and two copies of any attachments.

Step 4: Fax the letter and all documents (keep the fax confirmation sheet for your records).

Step 5: Staple the original attachments to a copy of your letter and save it for your files. (Send original letters but never send original receipts or other original documents.)

Step 6: Properly address two envelopes with the correct return address but do not put stamps on them!

Step 7: Staple one set of the attachment copies to your original letter and place it in envelope #1.

Step 8: Staple one set of attachment copies to a copy of your original letter and place it in envelope #2.

Step 9: Take both letters to the post office and follow the mailing instructions.

Mailing Instructions:

Envelope #1: Take the letter and attachments to the Post Office and send it by Certified Mail. Make sure to keep the cash receipt stamped with the amount and date and place it in a file marked "Credit disputes". The receipt should have the routing number on it.

Envelope #2: Take the letter and attachments to the Post Office and have them send it by first-class mail using "certificate of mailing". Keep the dated/stamped cash receipt and place it in a file marked "Credit Disputes". The receipt should also have the routing number on it.

Maintaining Proof of your actions

It is important to keep accurate records of all communication with creditors, debt collectors, and credit reporting agencies. This includes keeping copies of all letters, envelopes, and receipts to use as proof if needed.

For each letter you send, make sure to keep a copy of the creditor, debt collector, or credit reporting agency letter, the envelope that the documents came in, a copy of your signed letter with attachments stapled to it, a fax confirmation sheet, and a dated/stamped cash receipt from the Post Office for both envelopes #1 and #2.

By keeping these records, you can provide evidence in case of any legal disputes or complaints that may arise. It is important to keep these records organized and easily accessible.

Place all of these in a folder marked "Credit Disputes" and file away In a safe place for at least 15 years. Check the Statute of Limitations to see if you should keep the records longer.

Phone Logs

When dealing with debt and credit issues, it's important to keep a record of any phone conversations you have with creditors, debt collectors, credit reporting agencies, and other related parties. This is where a phone log can be very helpful. By logging the details of each call, you can keep track of who you spoke with, when the call was made or received, what was discussed during the call, and any other important information that was shared.

Having a clear idea of what you plan to say and any payment plans you may have in mind before making a call can also be very helpful. This will help you stay focused and on track during the call and ensure that you get all the information you need. Additionally, if you have a payment plan in mind, it can show the creditor or debt collector that you are taking your debt seriously and are committed to paying it off.

The free sample phone log provided can serve as a template for logging your phone calls. However, you can also develop your own phone log format that works best for you. The most important thing is to keep track of all your phone conversations to help you stay organized and ensure that you have a record of all the important details.

Company Name:	Company Address:
Phone No:	
Fax:	
Type of Account:	Account No:
Payment Due Date:	Regular Payment Amount:
Amount Past Due:	Reduced Payment Amount:
Record Calls Below:	
Date of Call:	Time Called:
Name of Person I Spoke with:	
Main Points of Conversation:	
Followup Date:	Notes:

The Arsenal

The weapons to defend yourself and fight back

The Arsenal

these are pre-written letter for every scenarios

The Arsenal section of the book is designed to provide you with pre-written letters for every situation you may encounter while dealing with debt and credit issues. With a collection of 12 sample letters, this section guides you on how to fight back and take control of your finances.

When communicating with creditors, debt collection companies, or junk debt buyers, it is crucial to start by sending them a letter requesting validation of the debt. Once you have sent the validation letter, you have the option to follow the left side of the chart below to continue negotiating a settlement in full or making payments. Alternatively, if you wish to dispute the debt, you may choose to follow the right side of the chart. This includes letters to send to new debt collectors, as they are likely to have the debt collector or junk debt buyer cease all communications with you and sell the account to someone else.

With the pre-written letters provided in The Arsenal, you have a clear path to follow and can take control of your financial situation. Whether you need to request a payment plan or dispute a debt, these letters will guide you through the process and help you achieve your financial goals.

Validation Letter

Date: (Today's Date)

(insert Collection Company
name and Full Address)

Re: Acct # (Insert Their referenced Account number
and original creditor company name)

To Whom It May Concern,

This letter is being sent to you in response to a notice sent to me on _____. This is a notice sent, pursuant to the (Insert State or Province) Consumer Protection Act, that your claim is disputed and validation is requested as I do not believe I owe what you say I owe.

This is a request for validation of the above debt. In accordance with the Act, I have the right to request for a validation of my debt. This is asking for proof regarding this and verifying the same.

Please attach copies of the following with the reply:
1. The agreement which authorizes the creditor to collect debt on the alleged debt.
2. The signed agreement from the debtor conforming to pay the creditor
3. The documents regarding the payments made on this account validating the amount.

If your office fails to respond to this request within 30 days from the date of receipt, all references to this account must be completely removed from my credit file and a copy of such deletion request must be sent to me immediately.

I would also like to request to you, in writing, that no telephone contact be made by your offices to my home or to my place of employment, under my right according to the (insert State or Province) Consumer Protection Act. All future communications with me must be done in writing and sent to the address below.

I am advising you to make sure that your records are in order or I will be forced to notify the proper authorities and take action against you.

Respectfully,
(your Signature & Name)
(Insert Your Mailing Address)

Debt Settlement Letter

A debt settlement letter is a formal letter that you can use to negotiate a settlement with a creditor or debt collector. It is a request to the creditor or collector to accept a lower amount than what is currently owed as full payment for a debt. Debt settlement is a useful tool for those struggling to repay their debts as it can allow them to avoid or end litigation, reduce their overall debt burden, and create a pathway to financial stability.

In this letter, you will need to clearly state your intention to settle the debt and the proposed amount you are willing to pay. Be sure to outline any financial difficulties you have been facing that make it difficult to pay the full amount owed. It's also important to highlight the benefits of accepting your settlement offer, such as avoiding lengthy and costly legal proceedings.

It is important to ensure that the terms of the settlement agreement are clearly stated in the letter, including the agreed upon amount and the date by which the payment must be made. This will help prevent any confusion or misunderstandings in the future.

Remember, debt settlement is a negotiation process, and it's important to approach it with a clear and professional mindset. Be respectful in your communication with the creditor or collector and remain firm in your offer while also being open to compromise.

Overall, a well-written debt settlement letter can be an effective tool to help you manage your debts and get your finances back on track. By taking the time to carefully craft your letter and thoughtfully negotiate with creditors or collectors, you can achieve a mutually beneficial outcome and move towards a brighter financial future.

Debt Settlement Letter

Date: (Today's Date)

(insert Collection Company
name and Full Address)

RE: Reference # (Their Reference number, if any)

Dear Collector,

I do not agree that I owe as much as you claim I owe on the above referenced account. In an effort to save both of us a great deal of time and expense I am offering to settle this account for $_____.

If you accept my offer, please send written confirmation to my address listed above. Once I receive your written confirmation, I will mail payment to your organization within five (5) business days. If you wish to discuss this settlement offer, I can be reached at (insert daytime phone number with area code). However, please understand that I will not make any payment until receiving written confirmation that you accept my offer.

Sincerely,

(your Signature & Name)

(insert Your Mailing Address)
Alternative Text:

I do not agree that I owe as much as you claim I owe on the above referenced account. In an effort to save both of us a great deal of time and expense I am offering to settle this account by making payments in the amount of $_____
every month (week or two weeks) for _____ Months totaling $_____.

Send this Debt Settlement Letter via "registered mail" and keep a copy for your records.

Paid in Full Letter

If you're making your final payment to a debt collection agency, it's important to have a record of your actions. When you come to the last payment on your debts, it's a good idea to send collectors a letter informing them of your final payment. This provides a written record of your actions and can help your case down the road should the matter come up again.

The paid in full letter is a letter you send to a debt collector or creditor to confirm that you have paid the entire balance owed on a debt. This letter serves as proof that the debt has been paid in full and should be sent after the final payment has been made.

The letter should include the following information:

- Your name and address
- The name and address of the debt collector or creditor
- The date of the final payment
- The total amount of the final payment
- The account number or reference number for the debt
- A statement that the debt has been paid in full
- A request for written confirmation of the paid in full status

By sending this letter, you are protecting yourself from any potential legal actions by the debt collector or creditor. It is also a good idea to keep a copy of the letter and any response you receive for your records.

Remember to always keep a record of all payments made, including the date, amount, and method of payment. This will help you keep track of your progress and ensure that you have a solid record of your actions in case you need it in the future.

Paid in Full Letter

Date: (Today's Date)

(insert Collection Company
name and Full Address)

RE: Reference # (Their Reference number, if any)

Dear Collector,

You'll find my final payment on the above referenced account enclosed. I request written confirmation showing this account as (paid in full or settled) according to our agreement on (insert date of agreement). However, should you choose not to provide me with confirmation, I will use your acceptance of this final payment as proof that you agree the account is (paid in full or settled).

Now that this debt is paid, I do not expect to hear from you except to confirm the account is paid. I will consider any other contact from you or your company as harassment and will immediately report your actions to the proper authorities and if necessary, take whatever legal action is necessary to protect myself. Finally, I expect you to remove this account and all references to my personal information from your records.

Respectfully,

(your Signature & Name)

(insert Your Mailing Address)

Send your Paid in Full letter via "registered mall" and keep a copy for your records

Debt Payment Agreement Letter

If you are struggling to meet the payment demands of a debt collector, you may feel overwhelmed and unsure of what to do next. In such cases, it's important to remember that you have options. One option is to negotiate a payment agreement that works for you and your financial situation. This can help you avoid defaulting on the debt and further damaging your credit score.

To do this, you can send a Debt Payment Agreement Letter to the collector, explaining your situation and proposing a payment plan that fits your budget. In the letter, be clear about how much you can afford to pay and how often you can make payments. You should also include the date when you will make your first payment, and any other details that are relevant to the agreement.

Keep in mind that the collector may not agree to your proposed payment plan, but it's important to try. If they do agree, make sure to get the agreement in writing and keep a copy for your records. This way, you have a record of the agreement in case any issues arise in the future.

By negotiating a payment agreement, you are taking control of your finances and showing the collector that you are willing to work towards resolving the debt. This can help improve your overall financial situation and reduce the stress and anxiety that comes with dealing with debt collectors.

Debt Payment Agreement Letter

Date: (Today's Date)

(insert Collection Company
name and Full Address)

RE: Reference # (Their Reference number, if any)

Dear Collector,

According to my records and your (phone call or letter) the balance of this debt is $_____. I am not disputing this debt however; my current financial situation prohibits me from paying the amount you're demanding. I am able to make payments on this account every (Insert date of month) to your company in
the amount of $_____.

I would appreciate a call from you confirming your acceptance of my payment terms. However, if I do not hear from you, I will consider your cashing or depositing my check as confirmation that you accept my payment terms. If you do not accept my terms then I expect the encased payment to be returned to me immediately in the enclosed self-addressed stamped envelope.

As a show of good faith I've enclosed my first payment in the amount of $_____.
If my financial situation improves enough for me to increase my payment amount I will contact you immediately.

Thank you for your understanding.

Sincerely,

(your Signature & Name)

(insert Your Mailing Address)

Send this Debt Payment Agreement via "registered mall" and keep a copy for your records.

Final Payment Warning Letter

If you're about to make your last payment and want to ensure that the creditor or collector knows it's your final payment, simply marking "Final Payment" or "Paid in Full" on your check may not be legally sufficient to relieve you of the debt if the creditor or collector claims the account still has a balance. To avoid any potential issues, consider sending a letter that informs the creditor or collector that you intend to send a final payment in thirty days. If you don't receive a response within that time frame, you can assume the creditor or collector agrees with you.

By sending in your final payment marked "Paid in Full" and ensuring the creditor or collector doesn't respond but cashes your payment, you'll be on solid ground should they decide to take you to court. However, it's important to act in good faith and only send a final payment warning when you truly believe your next payment will pay off the debt.

Note that if you owe $1,000 and send a payment of $10.00 marked "Paid in Full," this is not an ethical or effective approach. Instead, ensure that you can fulfill the terms of the final payment warning you send.

Final Payment Warning Letter

Date: (Today's Date)

(insert Collection Company
name and Full Address)

RE: Reference # (Their Reference number, if any)

Dear Collector,

My records show the balance on the above referenced account to be $_____.
This letter is to inform you that in 30 days from the date of this letter I intend to send a final payment for the exact amount and mark the instrument "Paid in Full".

If you disagree with my calculations, I expect to receive written explanation from you before 30 days otherwise I will assume you agree with my calculations and will accept my final payment and, after cashing my final payment show my account as zero balance. If you have any questions concerning this matter, I can be reached at (insert daytime phone number and area code).

Respectfully,

(your Signature & Name)

(insert Your Mailing Address)

Payment Refusal and Termination Letter

You have been making regular payments to a collection agency or a specific debt collector, but they have suddenly refused to accept your payment amount and are demanding that you pay a higher amount that you cannot afford. In this situation, you can send a sample letter to warn the collection agency or debt collector that, due to their refusal to accept your payment according to the previous agreement, you have no choice but to terminate the relationship.

When the collection agency receives this letter, they will likely reconsider their decision and continue with the original payment agreement. However, depending on the outstanding amount, they may choose to take legal action against you instead. It's important to note that you should welcome the opportunity to go to court since you have acted in good faith and documented each step, including negotiating and agreeing to a payment plan.

Payment Refusal and Termination Letter

Date: (Today's Date)

(insert Collection Company
name and Full Address)

RE: Reference # (Their Reference number, if any)

Dear Collector,

I have paid on this account per our agreement dated (insert date of verbal or written agreement). My records indicate that I have made (insert number) payments in the amount/s of $ _____ for a total of $ _____ in payments leaving a balance of $ _____.

Although I certainly want to continue paying on this debt, I simply cannot afford to pay the amount you are now demanding so, per your (phone call or letter) informing me that you refuse to accept my payments,

you leave me no choice but to terminate our relationship. For the record, do not contact me again regarding this account unless it is to inform me that my previous
payment offer is acceptable or that you intend to take other actions.

Should you decide that some type of legal action is necessary, be advised that I welcome the opportunity to show any judge my efforts to resolve this issue. I have kept extremely accurate records of all correspondence and payments, and therefore, have complete confidence that any court would agree that my efforts have been in good faith.

Respectfully,

(your Signature & Name)

(insert Your Mailing Address)

IMPORTANT: Always send Payment Refusal and Termination letters by "registered mall" and keep a copy for your records.

Debt Dispute Letter #1

Date: (Today's Date)

(insert Collection Company
name and Full Address)

RE: Reference # (Their Reference number, if any)

Dear Collector,

I am writing in response to your letter (letter or phone call) date (insert date), copy enclosed) because I do not believe I owe what you say I owe.

This is the first I've heard from you or any other company on this matter therefore, in accordance with the (Insert state or Provincial) Consumer Protection guidelines, I respectfully request that you provide me the following information:
- The amount of the debt;
- The name of the creditor to whom the debt is owed;
- Provide a verification or copy of any judgment (if applicable):
- Proof that you are licensed to collect debts in (your province)

Be advised that I am fully aware of my rights under (your provincial Consumer guidelines). For instance I know that:
- Because I have disputed in writing within 30 days of receipt of your dunning notice, you must obtain verification of the debt or a copy of the judgment against me and mail these items to me at your expense;

- You cannot add interest of fees except those allowed by the original contract or (state or provincial) law;
- You do not have to respond to this dispute but if you do, any attempt to collect this debt without validating it, violates the (State or Provincial) Consumer guidelines.

Also be advised that I am keeping very accurate records of all correspondence from you and your company including recording all phone calls and I will not hesitate to report violations of the law to the appropriate authorities.

I have disputed this debt, until validated you know your information concerning this debt is inaccurate. Thus if you already reported this debt to any credit-reporting agency or Credit Bureau then you must immediately inform them of any dispute with this debt. Reporting information that you know to be inaccurate or failing to report information correctly violates the Consumer Protection guidelines.

Should you pursue a judgment without validating this debt, I will inform the judge and request that the case be dismissed based on your failure to comply with the (your State or Provincial) Consumer guidelines.

Finally, if you do not own this debt, I demand that you immediately send a copy of this dispute letter to the original creditor so they are also aware of my dispute with this debt.

Respectfully,

(your Signature & Name)

(insert Your Mailing Address)

IMPORTANT: Always send Debt Dispute Letters by "registered mall" and keep a copy for your records.

Debt Dispute Letter #2

Date: (Today's Date)
(insert Collection Company
name and Full Address)
RE: Reference # (Their Reference number, if any)

Dear Collector,

I am writing in response to your letter (letter or phone call) dated (insert date of letter or phone call), (copy enclosed).

On (insert date of initial dispute letter), I sent you a letter explaining that I do not believe I owe what you say I owe. I must remind you that in my previous letter I requested the following information:
The amount of the debt;
The name of the creditor to whom the debt is owed;
Provide a verification or copy of any judgment (if applicable);
Proof that you are licensed to collect debt in (your province)

I also requested that if you have reported me to any credit reporting agency, that you inform them that I have placed this debt in dispute and to provide me with proof that you have done so. Furthermore, I asked that you immediately send me a copy of that dispute letter to the company (creditor) that you say i owe money to so they are also aware of my dispute with this debt.

As of today you have failed to respond to my request. For your convenience, I have included a copy of my previous letter and a copy of the mail receipt showing that you received my letter on (insert date from mail receipt). Since you have failed to respond I assume that you have been unable to validate the debt therefore, I consider this matter closed. You may consider this letter your official notification that I do not intend to correspond with you on this matter again unless you comply with my request.

I must remind you that any attempt to collect this debt without validating it, violates the (insert your state or province) Consumer Protection guidelines and that I am recording all phone calls and keeping all correspondence concerning this matter. Be advised that will not hesitate to report violations of the law to the proper
authorities.
Sincerely,

(your Signature & Name)

Debt Dispute for New Collector

You have previously disputed a debt, but you never heard back from the collector. Now, another collector is demanding payment from you. Due to the large number of delinquent accounts in North America, it is not uncommon for credit account records to become lost, destroyed, deleted, or misplaced. This makes it difficult for collectors to properly validate a debt, and when they cannot validate it, they often sell it to other collectors without informing you. This action is not a violation of Consumer Protection guidelines because debt collectors are not required to respond to a dispute unless they intend to validate the debt or take other specified actions allowed by law. If you need to dispute a debt again with a different collector, use the sample letter provided below, which contains the opening paragraph, and then continue with the body as provided in Sample Letter #1.

Date: (Today's Date)

(insert Collection Company
name and Full Address)

RE: Reference # (Their Reference number, if any)

Dear Collector,

I am writing in response to your letter (letter or phone call) date (insert date), (copy enclosed) because I do not believe I owe what you say I owe.

This is the (insert proper number) time I've disputed this debt. The first dispute was on (insert date) with (name of collection agency) and the second was on (insert date) with (insert name of collection agency). Be advised that neither collection agency responded to my dispute.

(Continue with body of Debt Dispute Letter #1)

Previously Settled Debt Letter

You've already settled a debt, but now a different collector is demanding payment. Given the millions of delinquent accounts being sold on the junk debt buyer (JDB) market, mistakes are bound to happen. In fact, every day, people receive phone calls from collectors demanding payment on accounts that were settled (paid less than the full balance) months or even years ago. When this happens to you, consider sending the collector a letter that states the debt has already been settled.

Previously Settled Debt Letter

Date: (Today's Date)

(insert Collection Company
name and Full Address)

RE: Reference # (Their Reference number, if any)

Dear Collector,

This letter is to inform you that the account in question was settled on (insert date) with (insert name of collection agency). I have enclosed copies of the settlement letter and proof of payment. You now have proof that this debt is no longer collectible, therefore I demand that you remove this account, and all references to my personal information, from your records. I do not expect to hear from you again regarding this matter however, should you choose to ignore this notification, I will consider any contact not in accordance with the (name of State or Province) Consumer Protection guidelines, a serious violation of those guidelines, and will immediately report any violations to the proper authorities.

Respectfully,

(your Signature & Name)

Expired Statute of Limitations Letter

A collector has called demanding payment of an old debt, but there is a statute of limitations (S.O.L.), also known as "time barred," on the enforcement of such debts. Although the S.O.L. has expired, creditors and collectors may still attempt to collect the debt, but they cannot use legal actions such as judgments, liens, and wage garnishments to force you to pay.

If you choose not to pay the debt, you can save yourself and the creditor or collector time and money by sending a letter informing them of the expired statute of limitations and your intention to use it as your defense should they decide to pursue legal actions. This assumes that the debt is valid.

Expired Statute of Limitations Letter

Date: (Today's Date)

(insert Collection Company
name and Full Address)

RE: Reference # (Their Reference number, if any)

Dear Collector,

This letter is in response to your (date of letter) copy enclosed or (date of phone call), concerning the collection of the above referenced (account number).

I do not believe I owe what you say I owe therefore I dispute this debt. I am well aware of my rights under the (state or province) Consumer Protection guidelines so I hope to save us a great deal of time by letting you know that not only do I dispute the validity of this debt, I have also checked and verified that the Statute of Limitations for enforcing this type of debt through the courts in (name of state or province) has expired. Therefore, should you decide to pursue this matter in court I intend to inform the court of my dispute of this debt and of the "Statute of Limitations".

As this letter is your formal notification that I consider this matter closed and demand that you, or anyone affiliated with your company, stop contacting me regarding this or any other matter except to advise me that your debt collection efforts are being terminated or that you or the creditor are taking specific actions
allowed by the (state or province) Consumer Protection guidelines.

Respectfully,

(your Signature & Name)

IMPORTANT: If you do not dispute the debt, leave that out of your letter just be aware that without the statement, sending an expired Statute of Limitations letter implies the debt Is yours and is valid.

Credit Bureau Removal Letter

Date: (Today's Date)

(Insert Credit Bureau name
and full Address)

Account : (Account number of the debt listed on your report)

To Whom it May Concern,

This letter is a formal complaint that you are reporting inaccurate credit information.

I have noticed that you have included the below information falsely in my credit profile and I am aware of its damaging effects on my good credit standing. As you are no doubt aware, credit reporting laws ensure that bureaus report only accurate credit information. No doubt the inclusion of this inaccurate information is a mistake on either your or the reporting creditor's part. Because of the mistakes on my credit report, I have been wrongfully denied credit recently for a   (*insert credit type for which you were denied here)*, which was highly embarrassing and has negatively impacted my life.

(optional) With the proof I'm attaching to this letter, I'm sure you'll agree it needs to be removed as soon as possible.

The following information needs to be verified and deleted from my credit report as soon as possible:

CREDITOR AGENCY - account #123-34567-ABC

Please delete the above information as quickly as possible.

Sincerely,

(your Signature & Name)

(insert Your Mailing Address)

Credit Bureau Removal Follow up Letter

Date: (Today's Date)

(Insert Credit Bureau name
and full Address)

RE: Account : (Account number of the debt listed on your report)

To Whom it May Concern,

I am writing to dispute the account referenced above. I have disputed this account information as inaccurate with you, and you have come back to me and stated you were able to verify this debt. How is this possible? Under the laws of the (FDCPA in the US or Consumer Protection ACT in Canada) , I have contacted the collection agency myself and have been unable to get them to verify that this is indeed my debt.

I enclose copies of my requests to the collection agency, asking them to validate my debts, and the receipts showing that I sent these letter certified signature request. This debt is not mine and I was given no evidence of my obligation to pay this debt to this collection agency.

The (FDCPA in the US or Consumer Protection ACT in Canada) requires you to verify the validity of the item within 30 days. If the validity can not be verified, you are obligated by law to remove the item. There is a clear case of unverified debt here, and I urge you to remove this item before I am forced to take legal action.

In the event that you can not verify the item pursuant to the (FDCPA in the US or Consumer Protection ACT in Canada), and you continue to list the disputed item on my credit report I will find it necessary to sue you for actual damages and declaratory relief under the (FDCPA in the US or Consumer Protection ACT in Canada). According to this regulation, I may sue you in any qualified state, province or federal court, including small claims court in my area.

While I prefer not to litigate, I will use the courts as needed to enforce my rights under the (FDCPA in the US or Consumer Protection ACT in Canada).

I look forward to an uneventful resolution of this matter.

Sincerely,

(your Signature & Name)

(insert Your Mailing Address)

BONUS: Sample Opt-Out Letter

In order to stop junk mail and telemarketing calls you need to keep your personal credit report information private. The best way to do this is to send a written "opt-out" request to the national credit bureaus. Herein is a sample of that letter.

Date: (Today's Date)

(Insert Credit Bureau name
and full Address)

Dear Credit Bureau:

I request my name be removed from your marketing list. Here is the information you require:

FIRST, MIDDLE & LAST NAME
(List all name variations, including Jr., Sr., etc.)

CURRENT MAILING ADDRESS
PREVIOUS MAILING ADDRESS
(Fill in your previous mailing address if you have moved in the last 6 months)

SOCIAL SECURITY/SIN NUMBER

DATE OF BIRTH

Thank you for your prompt handling of my request.

Sincerely,

(your Signature & Name)

(insert Your Mailing Address & Telephone Number)

A Final Word

I hope this guide has been helpful to you when dealing with collection agencies and aggressive collectors. Our goal is help you level the playing field and protect yourself from those who assume you "don't know" and take advantage of your position. You might owe but, that does not make you a bad person.

If you find yourself in any position the letters contained herein describe, you may use the letter as a guideline and write your own. Send it to the collector or the agency with a "return receipt requested"and keep a copy for your files. Be sure to have a copy of every letter you write and receive. If the situation develops into a legal matter, you stand on solid ground as you can present documents that would support your side of the matter. Also, if the agency does enter the account on your credit report and you wish to have it removed, you will have a record of the events that took place to provide to the credit bureau with documented proof as to "why" it should be removed. (Never validated, Settled, Etc.)

Regarding the recording of your phone calls with collectors, Be sure to advise them that you are recording the conversation. Ask that they repeat their name and then ask if that is their real name or a "desk"name. Some collectors do not use their real names and prefer to use an alias. There is nothing that says you cannot record the conversation nor is there anything that says you cannot send correspondence and keep a file. The worst that could happen is that tif the matter did go to court, you can present a solid case on your behalf. A good rule of thumb is; "if it's not written down, it never happened".

A final reminder; The use of any information contained herein, including letters, instructions, scripts, opinions, suggerstions, advice, are at the user's own risk. You are strongly encouraged to consult with legal and financial professionals prior to making any decision that could have legal or financial consequences to you.

Warmest Regards,

S.J. Carson & A. C. Duquette

FREQUENTLY ASKED QUESTIONS

Q: I asked for validation of the debt but have not received a response. What do I do?

A: The collection agency or the collector has no obligation to provide you with a validation. You can write another letter, attach a copy of your validation request and ask for another one. You can also send one to the creditor. Make sure you do so by certified mail and keep the receipt and file it. Do not make any payments on an account you believe that you do not owe what the collector says you owe.

Q: Why is a Validation important?

A: Suppose the collector is asking you to pay an amount that is not correct. That amount will be entered on your credit report. Interest will be applied to an amount that is incorrect. If a judgment is entered against you, the amount of the judgment would be incorrect. You may have made payments that were not posted to your account or there could be the possibility that the creditor miscalculated interest applied. Hidden fees could be applied that you are not aware of. The debt might not even be your debt. You have a right to obtain validation of the debt. Exercise that right and get validation.

Q: Can the collector call my place of employment?

A: Yes. But the collector cannot ask any questions regarding salary. You may send a written request that the collector not call your employer in the future. Again, do so via certified mail and keep a copy and file it. In that letter you can also advise the collector that calling you at home is in-convenient and request that all contact is done via mail. Advise him that failure to comply will be viewed as harassment.

Q: Do I have to pay what the collector demands in order to avoid any legal action?

A: No, you do not. Pay what you can afford to pay. Make the collector an offer that you can comfortably afford. The collector cannot refuse payment if it is reasonable. Put your offer in writing and send via certified mail and keep a copy and file it. Ask for a written confirmation of acceptance in your letter. **DO NOT SEND PAYMENT** until it is agreed to by the collector. Then send the payment. **Do NOT** send a check, Send a money order.

Q: Can the collection agency sue me or garnish my pay-check?

A: Yes BUT...they must receive permission from the original creditor as the collection agency is a third party and they cannot take any legal action without permission from the creditor. Furthermore, the debt must be validated by a written affidavit stating that the money owed is a true and correct amount. Also, you must be served notice of the court action including the date.

Q: I had arrangements with one collector, now a different one is calling. What do I do?
A: In a letter, send a copy of the agreement you previously had with the other collector. Be sure to send it Registered and keep a copy.

Q: A collector is calling and demanding payment on a debt that over 4 years old. What can I do?

A: Chances are the debt was purchased by a junk debt buyer. Advise the collector that you do not believe you owe what they says you owe and offer a payment to settle the account. Remember, the account was purchased for pennies on the dollar and you can offer the same. Be sure if they agrees to obtain the agreement in writing and ask as part of the agreement that he notes the account on your credit report as "settled".

Q: I settled an account years ago. A collector keeps calling. How can I stop him from harassing me?

A: By Registered mail, send them a copy of the Paid-in-full or settled notice you received from the last collection agency. Advise them in the letter that you are requesting cease all further communication as your account has been paid. If you paid the creditor directly, get a confirmation from the creditor and send it to the collector with the same demand.

Q: A collector is calling and stating that they will attach legal action against my Mother's estate for a bill that hasn't been paid. Can they?

A: If the debt is past the statute of limitations, they cannot. Offer a settlement. If the debt is outside the limitations, they cannot use any legal remedy to collect the debt.

Q: I agreed to pay $50 a month on my account. Is that okay?

A: That's fine providing you have it in writing between you and the collector. If not, have the collector send you a letter confirming that arrangement. If another collector obtains your account, they would have no record of your agreement, All agreements should be in writing so you have proof.

Q: My credit card balance is $5,000.00 and I lost my job. How do I negotiate for a lower payment until I can catch up?

A: First, call your credit card company. Ask to speak with a Supervisor, Tell them your problem and ask if you can pay the principle amount minus the interest and you would like a period of time to clear the balance. Advise them that if you cannot do this, chances are that you will not be able to pay anything as you have other debt you are trying to work out. Then shut up. Say nothing. The credit card company knows that receiving something is better than nothing and they are likely to allow you to make the payment on the principle. Be sure you can, (This is the "short" Version).

Q: The debt collector tells me that I have to call the creditor for validation and when I call the creditor, they tell me that I need to speak with the collection agency. What do I do?

A: This is the "ping-pong" game. The creditor has the original file. The collection agency has a copy of that file which the creditor sent to them for collection activity. As the debt collector has no obligation to validate the debt, the real responsibility falls on the creditor. Write the creditor and ask for validation of the debt. They have it. Send the letter Registered and provide a time within you expect a reply. Keep a copy for your file. When the collector calls again, advise them that you are waiting on validation and until one is received, you will not discuss the matter further.

Q: I paid the debt but it still appears on my credit report as "outstanding". How do I get it removed?

A: Write the credit bureau and provide them with documentation that proves you paid the debt. Ask them to show the debt as either "paid" or "settled" depending on the circumstances. You must provide the credit bureau with proof that you have in fact paid the debt.

Q: Is there such thing as "debt elimination"?

A: Yes and No, Some accounts will stay on the credit report for 6 years as outstanding. Most bad debts that are on the credit report can be taken care of by settlement. Have the collector/creditor note the account after payment, "Paid", "Settled", "Disputed" etc. Those that are paid and or settled will not count against you as outstanding. Left alone they will remain as un-paid and lower your credit score and continue to show you as a credit risk. The only other way to "eliminate debt" is not to go into it to begin with.

www.ingramcontent.com/pod-product-compliance
Lightning Source LLC
Chambersburg PA
CBHW050330220526
45465CB00012B/637